Alaska's

PRINCE WILLIAM SOUND

Author and Photographer
Daryl Pederson

PUBLICATION CONSULTANTS
We Believe In The Power Of Authors
PO Box 221974 Anchorage, Alaska 99522-1974
books@publicationconsultants.com—www.publicationconsultants.com

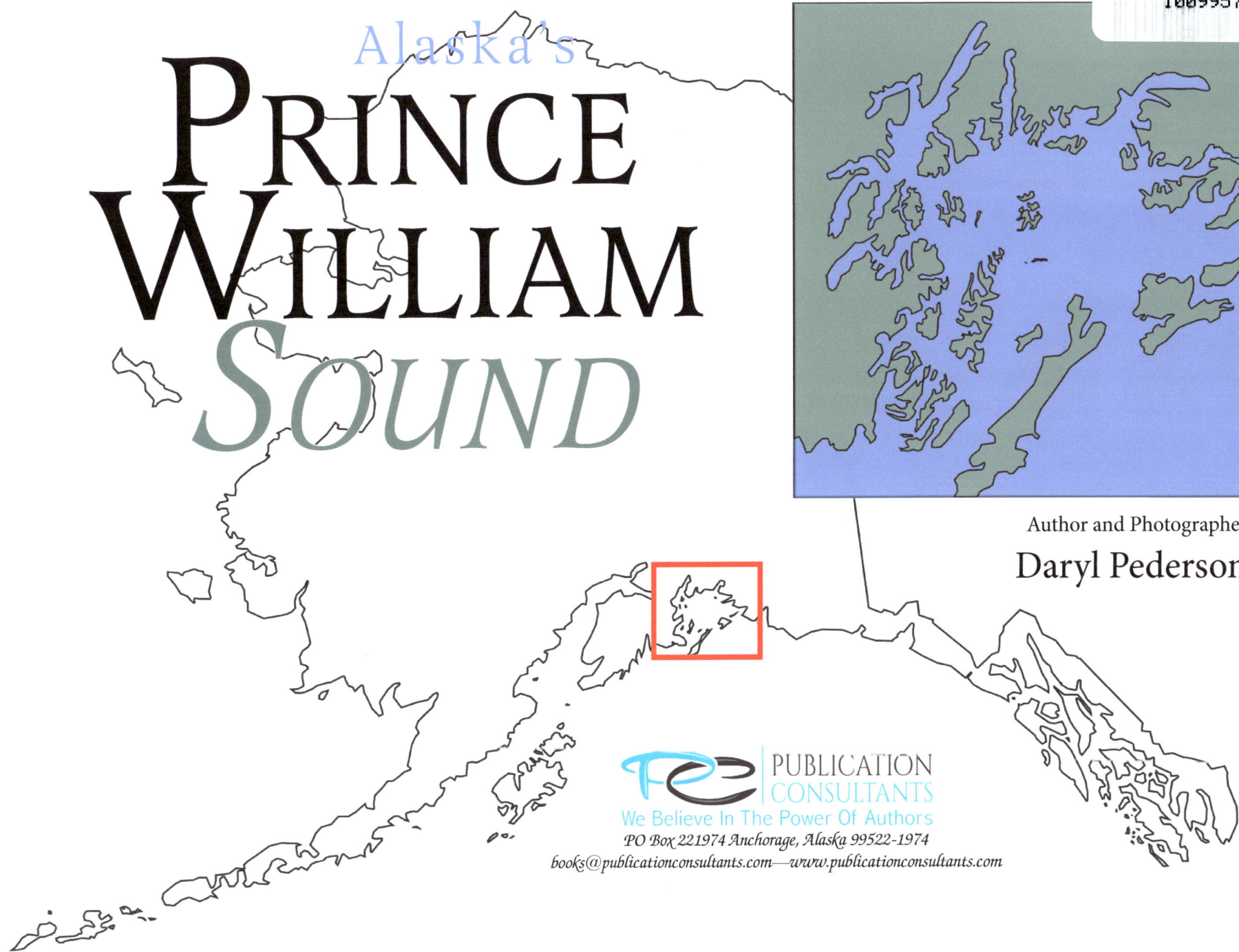

ISBN: 978-1-63747-018-3

Library of Congress Catalog Card Number: 2016951826

—Second Edition—

Deep water bay on a windless September morning.

Introduction

The Prince William Sound is a spectacular place on Earth. The confluence of the Ice Age and Climate change. Where the sights are heavenly, and the sounds divine: the bald eagles song as it soars beside a waterfall, or a spouting whale at sunset. Northern lights slow dancing to a changing tide, or a full sail run with Dall's porpoise in tow. Glaciers have their own powerful voice that commands attention, softened by the luster of blue icebergs that resemble gigantic sparkling gemstones. It's all here, stimulus overload for the eyes and ears.

I always think of the Sound as a her. Probably because it can either be a dream come true, or your worst nightmare. Sometimes both in the same day. It's heaven or hell depending on the weather. A region where function sustains life, and fashion goes to die. Good days are especially captivating with the allure of the Sounds' pristine

natural surroundings. The variety of scenic wonders are tremendous. Great days here are as good as this world gets. There is a certain spirit about these days that inspires love for both the water and the land. I have fallen in love with the Prince William Sound, and gladly take the bad with the good.

It rains hard here. So hard that it dents the Ocean. The wind is capable of either changing your life or ending it. I have watched 100mph gusts throw waterfalls back up mountains. The combination of the two is an awe-inspiring force, and a potential recipe for disaster. I've gone to sleep in a tent, climbing into a soggy sleeping bag wearing neoprene chest waders to stave off hypothermia, and watched from this portable shelter for days as whole mountains became white with falling water. The expected time for the arrival of these storms in the past was a bit less predictable, today's technology aids in decision making when setting out on a course for adventure. Beware. Forecasts aren't always accurate. Experience is for hire all around the Sound, and highly recommended to insure safety for newcomers.

The rough days make an impression, however, what I remember vividly are the great days. Fortunately I have had more than most. With 20 plus hours of light at the peak of summer, extended play is a daily occurrence. Oftentimes my excursions start at 5am, and go until midnight. There will be time to catch up on sleep during the winter. Decades of learning has given me an education. With a boat, a few skills, and knowledge of the Sound, I have been able to chase hard in the pursuit of happiness. Each of these photographs convey a story, and represent a memorable moment in time. The pictures are my trophies, a reward for plenty of effort, yet above all, the experiences I have had are what make life grand. Everyone has their own happy place: for that, the Prince William Sound is mine.

~DARYL PEDERSON

The Prince William Sound

Sound /sound/ noun

a sound is a coastal waterway that
connects in two or more places,
to one or more bodies of water.

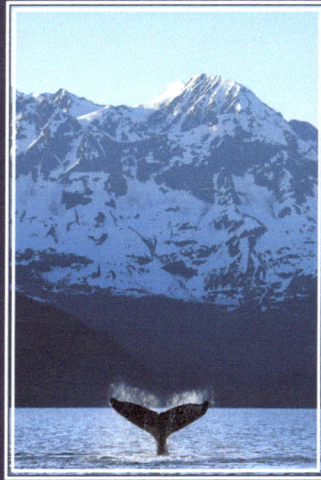

A Waterway of Life

With water comes life. From the Gulf of Alaska, to its furthest reaches with its plunging depths, the Prince William sound is alive. A few hundred species of birds, thirty land, and a dozen marine mammals, thrive in its environment. People are here too, as they have been for untold numbers of years. Early inhabitants were drawn to its abundant food and fur sources in their struggle to exist. Since then others have found their way for a variety of reasons. Captain James Cook dropped anchor here in may of 1778, naming it Sandwich Sound. Map editors would later rename it Prince William Sound, to honor King George III, for his third son Prince William Henry. Subsequent to Cook's visit human activity increased greatly. Today places around the sound are named after the original inhabitants, as well as explorers and dignitaries from Russia, Spain, England, America, and Alaska.

3800 miles of coastline are predominately encompassed by the precipitous and glaciated Chugach mountain range. Most of the land includes the nearly seven million acre Chugach National Forest, America and Alaska's second largest designated national forest. Valdez is home to the largest port. Cordova and Whittier are the other main ports with harbor towns. Chenega, and Tatitlik make up the Alaskan native villages.

above Harvard Glacier, College fjord.   *right* A mother otter shares a clam with her young pup.

previous page The panoramic view across Wells passage of layered landscape making up the Kenai Peninsulas north eastern edge.   *right* Clear blue Iceberg, Barry Arm.   *below* Harlequin Ducks, Port Wells.

right A group of sea lions prepare to break the surface at Lone passage.
below A sport fisherman takes in a perfect day at Montague straights.

left Columbia glacier, Prince William
Sound's largest tidewater glacier.

right Harriman glacier and Fjord.

next pages Johnson bay at sunrise.

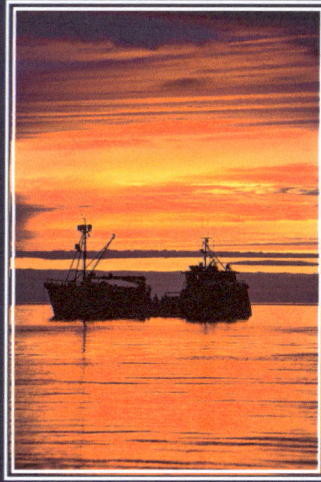

Sailor Take Warning

Mountains of the Kenai Peninsula and the Chugach Range, rising up over thirteen thousand feet, stop the clouds blowing in from the Gulf of Alaska and ring out their moisture. Then there's the wind. Where storms located in other places on earth are named hurricanes, Alaskans call them Saturday, ... or Tuesday, depending on the day of arrival. One hundred mile per hour winds are not uncommon around the sound during the fall and winter months. There's an upside. The purest air on earth is found here.

previous page Orca spouts at sunset, Dangerous passage.

left Horsetail clouds above Knight Island.

right Rain patterns on the ocean, Cochrane bay.

More than a couple centuries later the sound has avoided any dramatic growth in population. Mostly because of the weather. At its entrance, Montague island is the largest uninhabited island in the united states. Of the hundreds of other islands scattered around the sound, few include residents. Whittier's annual rain and snowfall average roughly two hundred inches each, making it the wettest city in the United States.

As Summer comes back around so do the people and things that depend on it for a living. Much of the wildlife, as well as most of the folks who make an income here are seasonal. Industries include oil, commercial and sport fishing, tourism, aqua-farming, and shipping. Along with the working, come those in search of recreation. Fishing is a favorite, along with kayaking, sightseeing, boating, hunting, camping, and hiking. There is truly something for everyone.

above Granite Bay and Mount Gilbert. *right* Breaching humpback whale, lower Herring Bay. *next page* Tufted Puffin, LaTouche Passage.

previous page A happy hook setter, Lone passage.

left A leisurely swimming smack
    of Moon Jellyfish, Culross Bay.

right A bald eagle tucks its wings to gain
    speed as it pursues a group of gulls.

previous Picturesque Bay living up to its name with a vivid September sunrise.
below Aerial view of Esther island and passage.

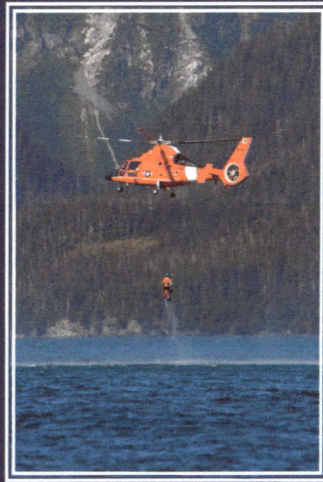

Sound Choices

Two roads, two airports, the Alaska Marine Highway, and the Alaska Railroad connect travelers to the Sound. After a fifty mile scenic drive from Anchorage along the Turnagain Arm, via the Seward highway, an east turn onto Portage glacier road will bring you to Maynard mountain. You then drive through the mountain. Anton Anderson Memorial Tunnel is the longest combined vehicle-railroad tunnel in North America. It provides access to the Sound at the head of Passage canal and the City of Whittier.

left Paddleboarder, Surprise glacier.

right Lucky Bay, Knight Island.

High mountains, with hanging glaciers and waterfalls make up a large portion of the Whittiers' panoramic views. The largest kittiwake rookery in the north pacific, together with numerous eagles, bold northwestern crow, great gray owls, Gulls, murre and murrelets, are some of the options for birders to enjoy. Land and sea otters, seals and sea lions, are often sighted as well. Occasionally humpback whales, and orcas, range around the six hundred foot deep waters of Passage canal. Glacier tours, sport fishing, kayak trips, and hiking are among the options that make Whittier a favorable choice for summer visitors. Built up by the US Army during WWII, and crushed down by the tsunamis associated with the gigantic 1964 earthquake, the year round population today is just over two hundred.

On the east side of the Sound, along the north shore of Port Valdez, is the city of Valdez. It is situated among spectacular towering mountains with a deep emerald fjord. Visiting requires either flying just over a hundred air miles from Anchorage, arriving by boat, or driving three hundred road miles to the southern end of the Richardson Highway. An ice free deep water port was connected to the heart of Alaska with the completion of the road in 1899. This enabled prosperous growth, making it the largest of the three cities located around the Prince William Sound. Roughly four thousand people reside here. The terminal for the Trans-Alaska pipeline was built here in the 1970's for tanker ships to transport oil. Valdez is a premier destination for sport fishing, scenic and glacier tours, hiking, photography, skiing, and lots of other recreation.

right A commercial seiner purses up a nice haul of Chum salmon, Wells passage.

left Glacial waterfall, Blackstone bay.

right A young Orca hops along as it navigates across Knight passage, with a beautiful background view of the Chugach mountains.

The city of Cordova is located along Orca Inlet, in the southeast section of Prince William Sound. Boat, or Airplane are your only options to get there, making this landlocked community most appealing for those not looking for a road, but a wilderness less traveled. An array of industry has come and gone, but commercial fishing here is famous. The most sought after salmon in the world are caught here; the Copper River strain.

Cordova is the birders paradise of anywhere in the Sound. Lots of other wildlife make a splash in these parts as well. They don't have a choice, it's wet here. If gray is your favorite color you will love this place. One hundred sixty inches of rain, and half as much in snow fall annually. Despite the weather more than twenty three hundred people currently reside in this cool maritime rainforest environment.

left A black bear forages in an alpine meadow.

right Commercial Sockeye salmon gillnetter.

left An aerial perspective reveals the art of nature, Bay of Isles.

right Eagle in the mist, Whittier.

The Sound has been here longer than we could know. In the brief period that journals, or recording devices have documented events, attention is given to the biggest stories of last hundred years. Life at the edge of any Ocean doesn't happen without occasional peril. There are risks for the reward of a living along the waterfront. This area is well know for two separate disastrous events. Whether natural or human-caused, catastrophes tend to put places on a map.

left The residents of Whittier deal with yet another severe winter wind event.

left Swift currents from a
changing tide, Hidden Bay.

right Chenega village with the
State ferry Tustamena.

left One hundred mile per hour gusts throw a waterfall back up a mountain.

right Tsunami debri cleanup effort.

The Chugach Alutiiq villages of Chenega, and Tatitlek, make up the other places with year round populations of close to one hundred people each. Both have endured seemingly insurmountable hardships, and moves. Centuries of history along with one third of its people were lost in an instant when a tsunami, created by the gigantic 1964 earthquack hit Chenega Island.. The village was reestablished 20 years later on Evans Island. Both of the villages subsistence lifestyles were devastated by the Exxon Valdez oil spill 25 years later.

left Crushed granite beaches can be
found throughout the Sound

right A Humpback whale
spouts in the late
evening hours,
Main bay

left The Bligh reef navigational marker shows where a number of ships have run aground, including the supertanker Exxon Valdez.

right Midnight at Ingot island

In 1989, the supertanker Exxon Valdez struck Bligh reef causing the second largest oil spill in US waters, severely impacting marine life in its path. Other ships have run aground here including the 180ft SS Olympia in 1910, and despite the installation of an automated navigation light, the tug Pathfinder collided into the reef in 2009.

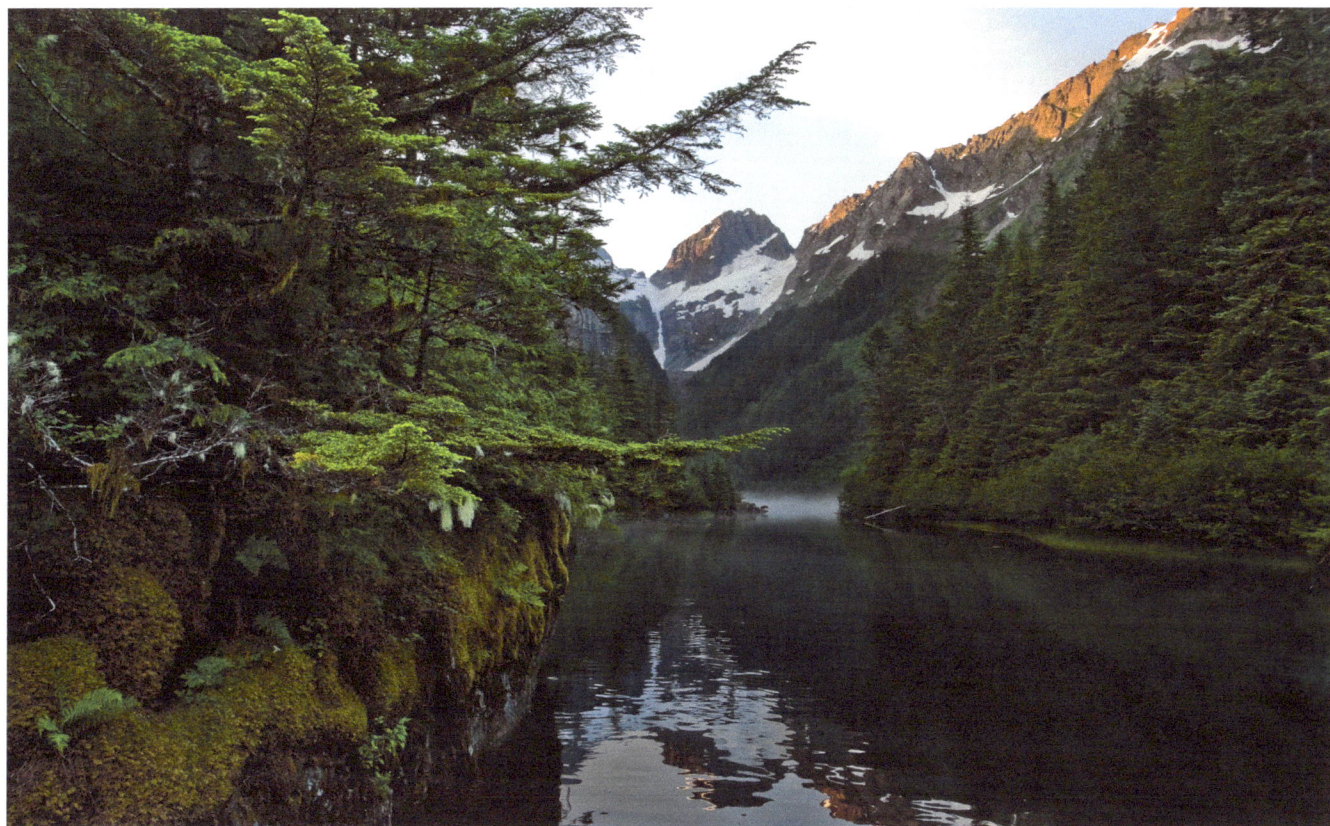

above There are bays around the sound only accessible by boat
during extreme high tides associated with lunar phases.

left Benoit glacier, a place where the Ice Age and climate change come together.

left Sundew; a carnivorous plant
absorbs a few pesky blackfly.

right A low flying Eagle, Johnson bay.

left Dock piles, Culross Island.

right Ore cart, western Prince William Sound.

next page A pod of Orcas gather for
a brief rest as they navigate
the waters of Perry passage.

The epicenter of the 1964 earthquake is located along the northern coast of the Prince William Sound. With a magnitude of 9.2 it was the largest ever recorded in US history. Many lives were lost on the east, west and south edges of the sound, all from tsunami waves. Its affects were felt around the world.

above Sea lions feast on pink salmon returning to Saw Mill Bay. streams tilt on edge, making unique and interesting patterns.

right Rocks caught in the middle of the beach break, and fresh water

left The Frank Lloyd Wright
waterfall at Hidden Bay.

right A lunge feeding humpback
whale surges above
the water, Olsen Island.

left Commercial fishing seiners,
Valdez Narrows.

right Skate's eye

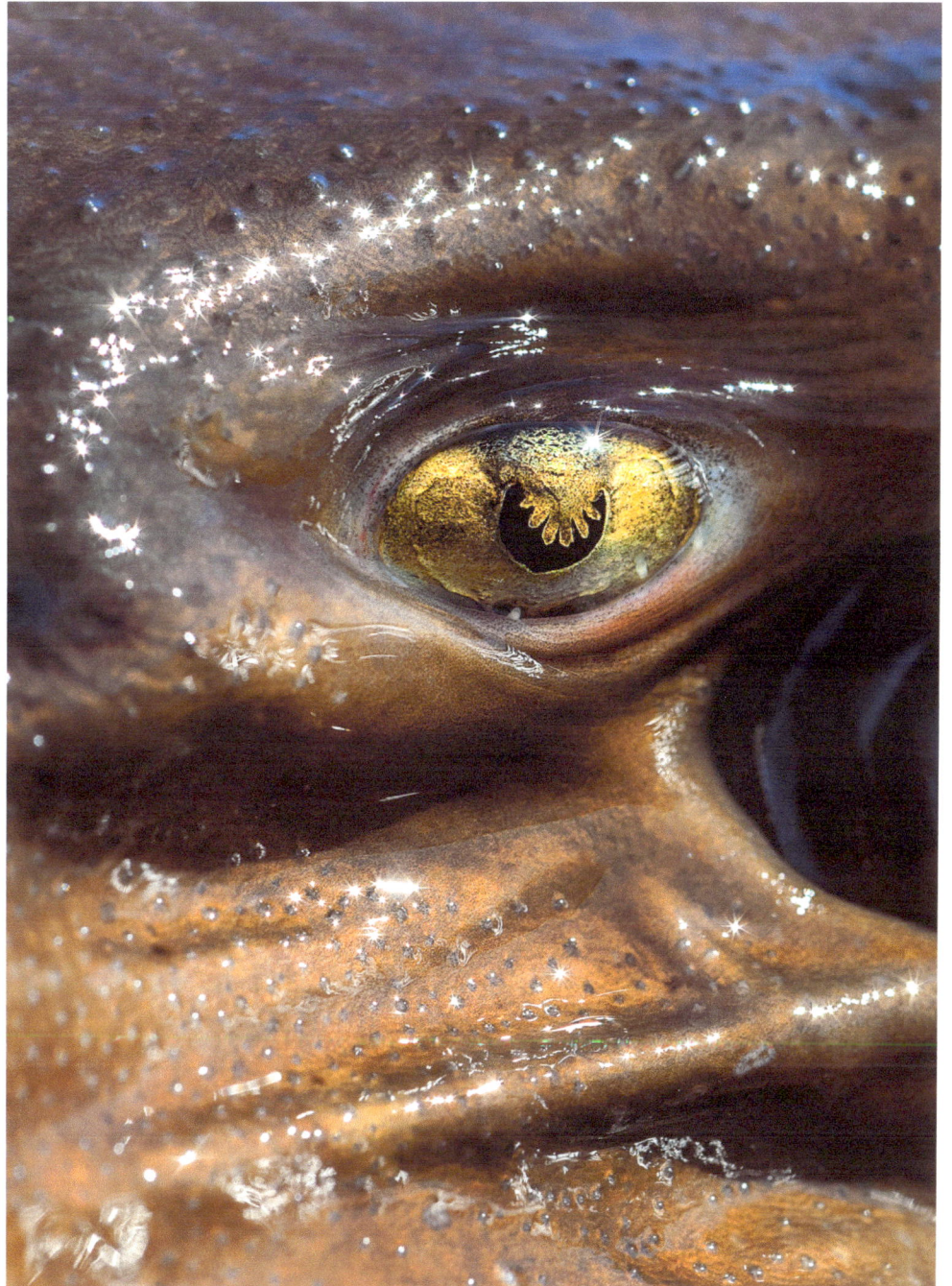

left Black legged Kittiwakes

right Dall's porpoise.

left A humpback whale at sunrise, Perry passage.   *below* Brown bear with Chum salmon, Olsen bay.

Alaska is home to a wide variety of natural beauty, making it difficult for me to commit to one particular destination. Love for the ocean and all its treasures makes the Sound choice easier. Wild and pure, vibrant and ever changing, there is a powerful attraction to this body of water. Spending time here is a gift. A photographer has a leg up here as beautiful places are photogenic. The past quarter century has been dreamy. To have done justice to this precious area with all its offerings to the world is to take you there with photographs, conveying the essence of the Prince William Sound; an extraordinary place on Earth.

left A humback performs for a passing seiner, Squire Island.   *next page* A sunrise feeding frenzy brings Humpback whales, sea lions, and Dall's porpoise together in a close group.

left A rare summer light pillar burns bright alongside lenticular clouds above Unakwik inlet.

right *F/V Gore Point* hauls in a purse of sockeye salmon at Shoestring Cove.

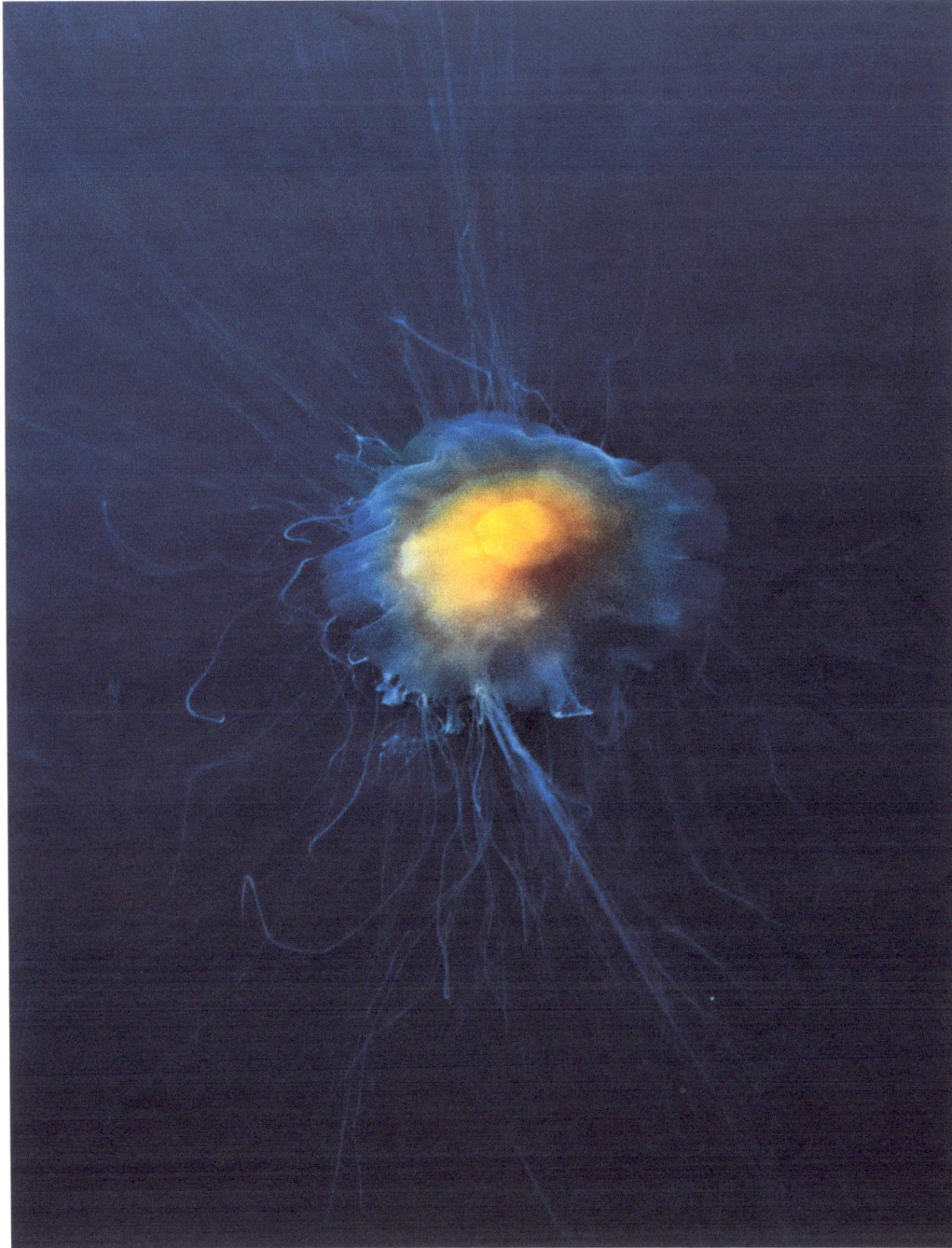

left Lion's mane Jellyfish.

right Knight Island's steep and
        rugged mountains.

next page West Twin bay sunset.

left Breaching Orca, Perry Island.

right A giant red octopus loses a
         battle with a sea otter.

left The Northern lights glow reflects on Main bay, on a windless September night.

right American bald eagle portrait, Italian bay.

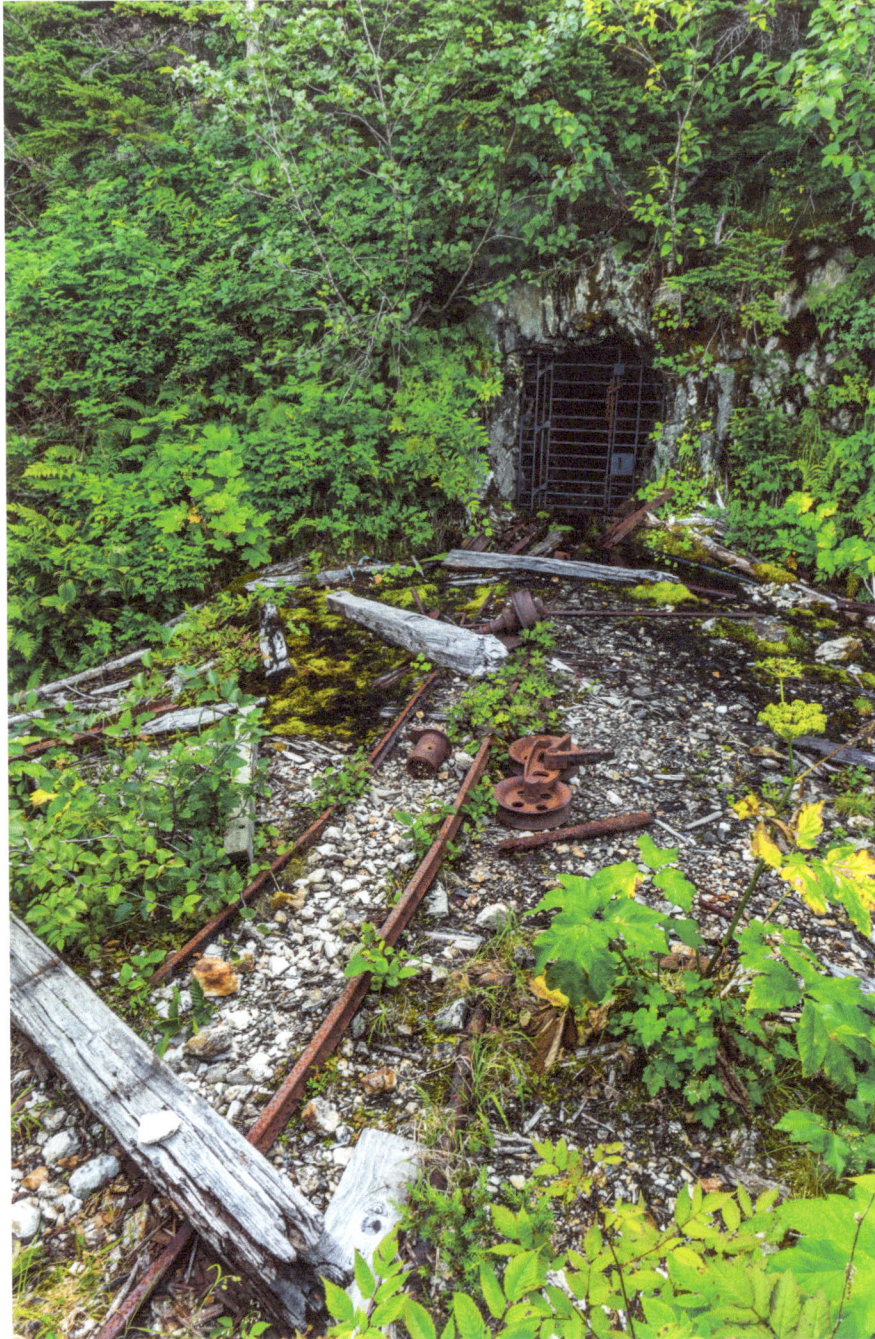

left The Prince William Sound
has a rich mining history.

right A few dozen Sitka blacktail deer
were transplanted on Hawkins,
and Hinchinbrook islands near
Cordova in the early 1900's.

They are exceptional swimmers
and have since populated most
of the major islands throughout
Prince William Sound.

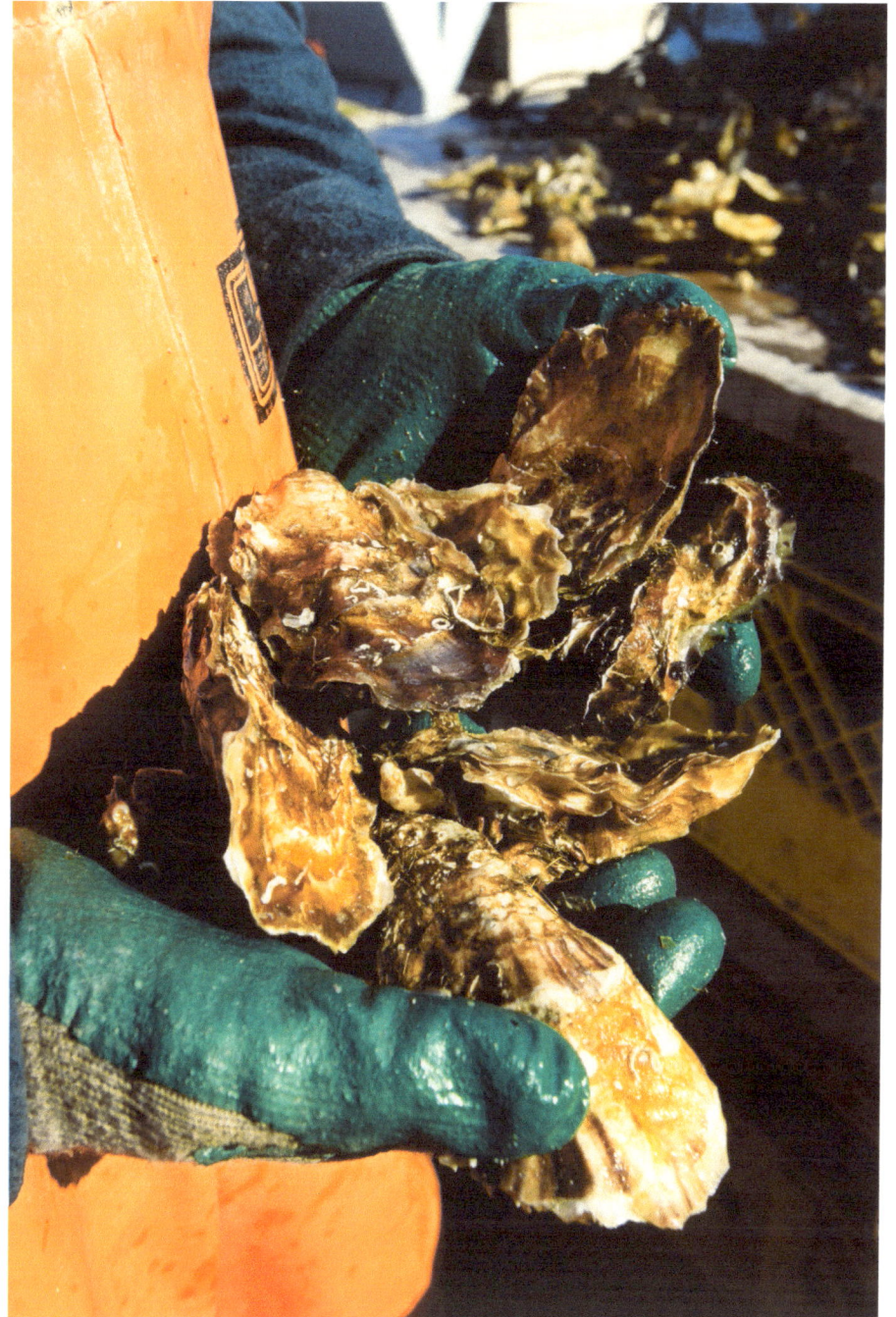

left A large baitball of fish hug the coastline of Rua cove.

right Alaskan Oysters.

next page Deep Water bay with its stunning granite domes.

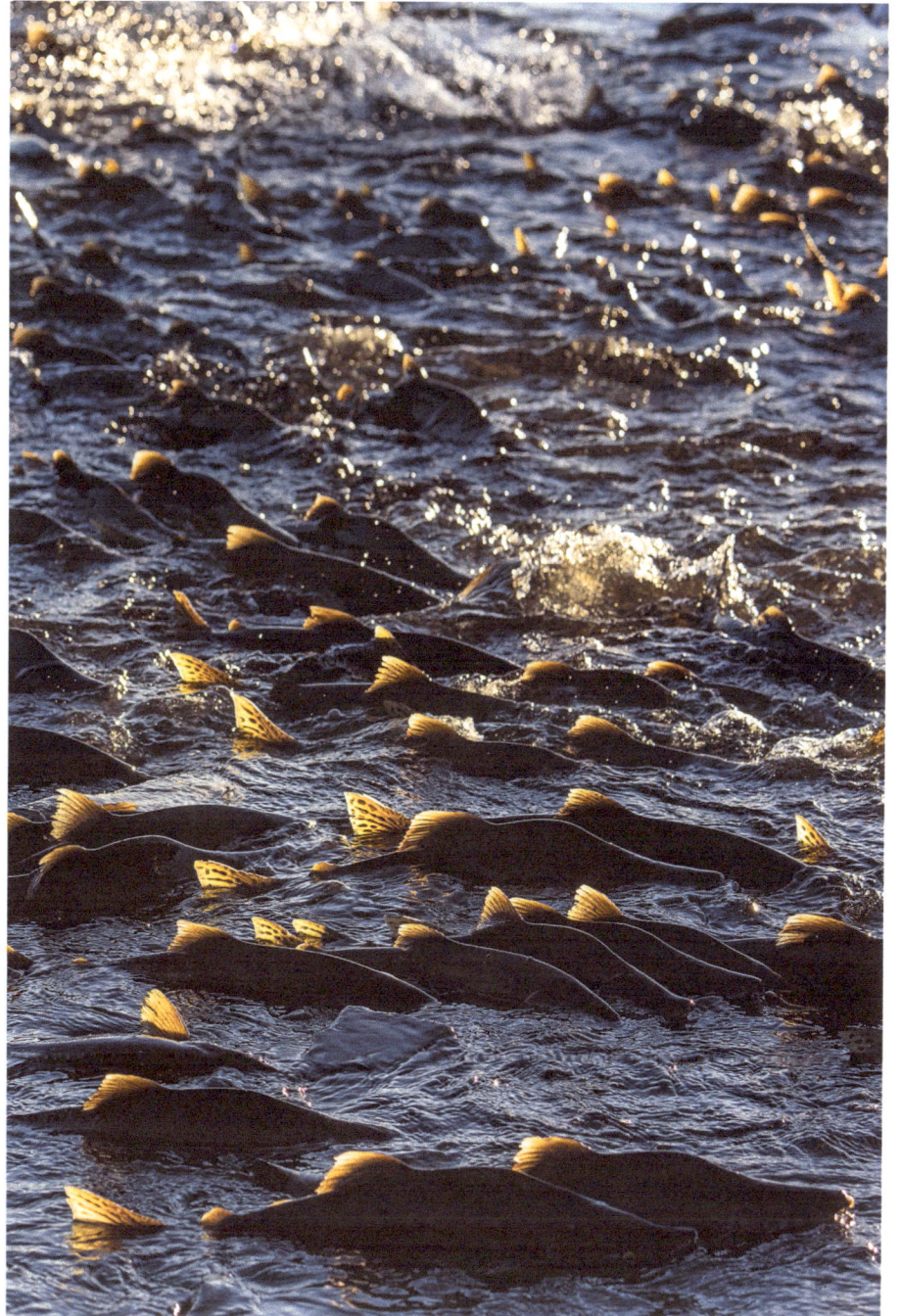

left Tidewater glacier, Columbia bay.

right Pink salmon stacking up at low tide near the AFK Hatchery.

left Spruce pollen, Perry passage.

right Forest fire smoke from interior
Alaska makes its way south
to Orca inlet at Cordova.

left A sport fisherman battles a sockeye salmon, Long bay

right Adapt and survive; in many areas of the Sound, trees maintain a low profile to live through the heavy winter snow conditions, and consistent hurricane force winds.

left If conditions are favorable the mist from whale spouts reflect rainbow colors.

right Some commercial fishing boats are more colorful than others.

left A fog bow is a similar phenomenon to a rainbow. Because of the very small size of water droplets that cause fog, colors are almost nonexistent.   *below* Aerial view of Esther Island, and the western Prince William Sound.

left Blueberries are one of many different types of berries that can be harvested throughout the Sound.

right An aerial view of Squire island and Long passage

left Northwestern Crow.

right An Oystercatcher searches
the coast of Eaglek bay.

next page Cruising at slower speeds will
occasionally attract playful porpoises.

left AFK Hatchery at Sawmill bay.

right At first glance this four foot long polychaete worm resembles a water snake as it wriggles along.

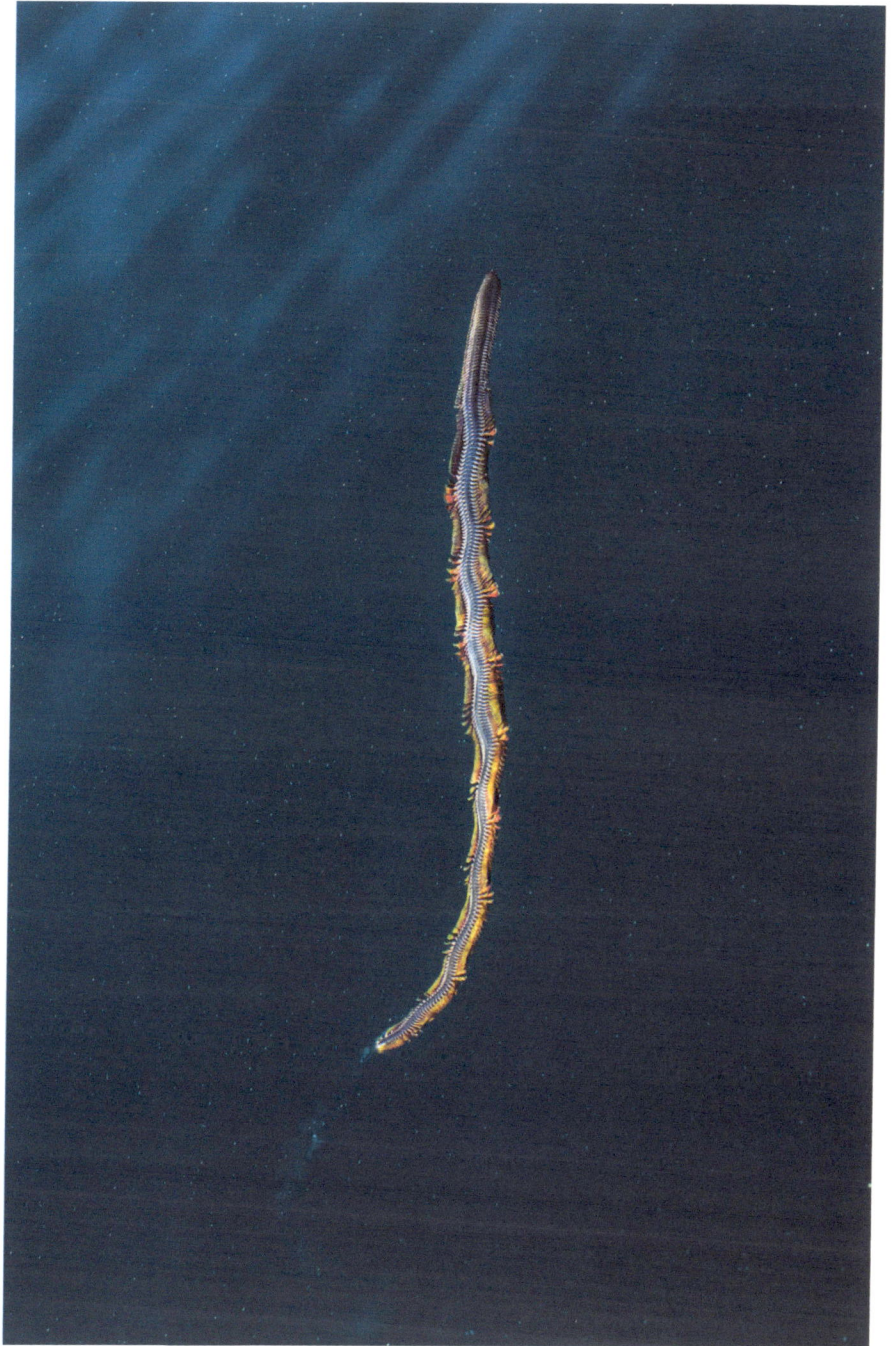

left Copper bay entrance, Knight Island.

right A floatplane delivers a guest to a recreational use cabin at Schrode lake.

left A perfectly symmetrical Humpback whale fluke, Crafton Island.

right A spring black bear takes a look around from its vantage point along Esther passage.

left A Bald Eagle picks up a meal as the sun sets behind Dangerous passage.

right A branded sea lion, rests among the local Esther rock inhabitants.

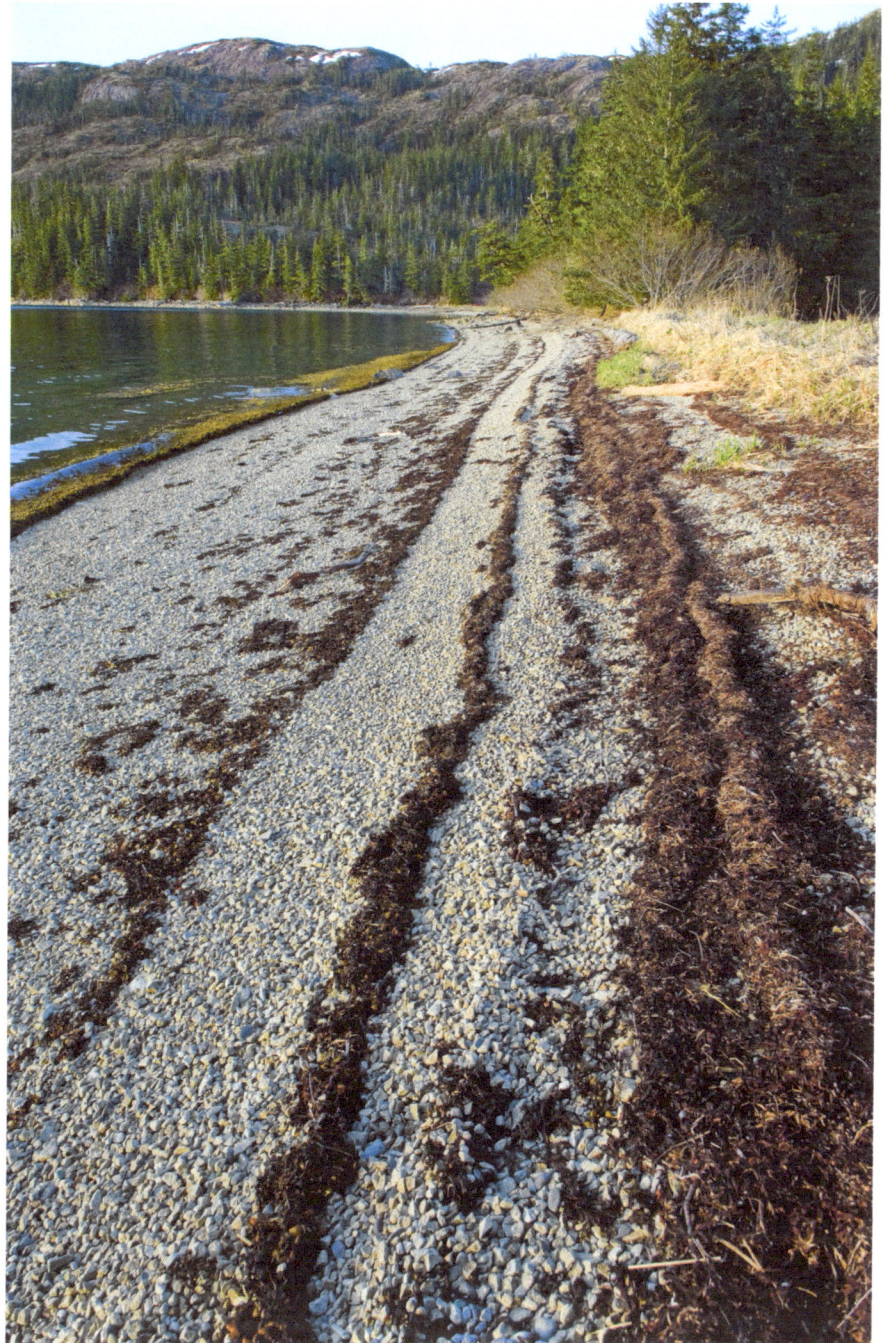

left Fata Morgana is a mirage consisting of multiple images, such as these islands with a large ship, that are seen in a narrow band above the horizon.

right Gently changing tides leave timelines on the island beaches.

left Talking Orca, Drier bay.

right Northern rainforest,
Esther island.

below Sea anemones hang along the edge of New Year island during an extreme low tide.   right A fog bow makes a full halo as it drifts by like a smoke ring.   next page A large raft of sea otters gathers in Orca inlet.

Daryl Pederson grew up in Sterling, Alaska, and for the last three decades has been an Anchorage-based nature and studio photographer. His most recent books are

The Northern Lights, celestial performances of the Aurora Borealis and *A is for Alaska*. Daryl's photographs can be seen worldwide hanging in offices, embassy, government buildings, and as cover shots for books and magazines, including *National Geographic*. More of his work can be viewed on his website, Alaskalight.com.

I dedicate this book to my daughters, Makena, and Amara, who I love more than they could ever know.